AF251199

UNDERSTANDING DULT LEARNERS

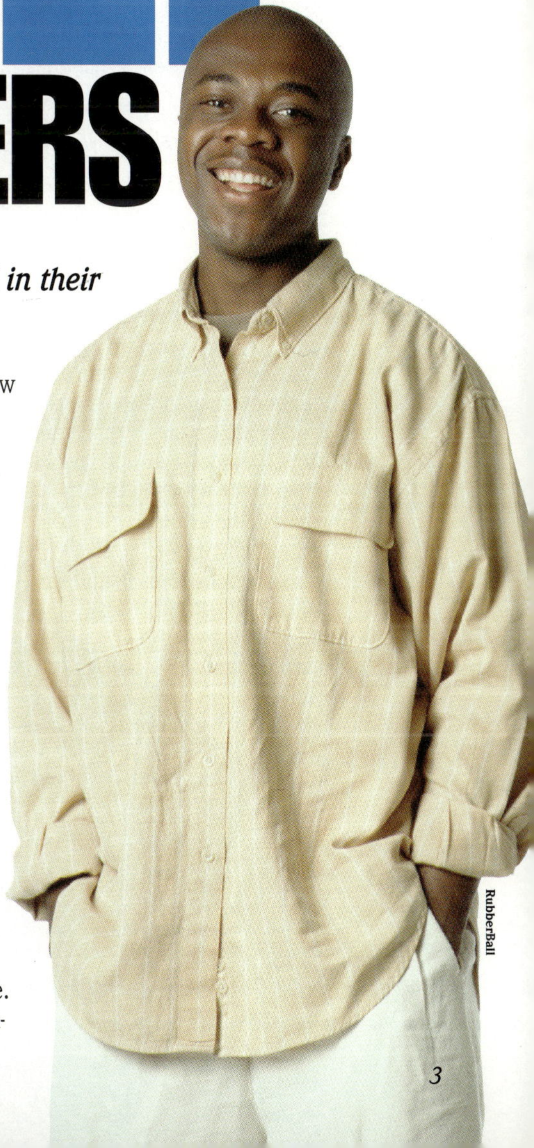

RubberBall

■ *Adults are more self-directed in their learning.*

Dynamic Graphics

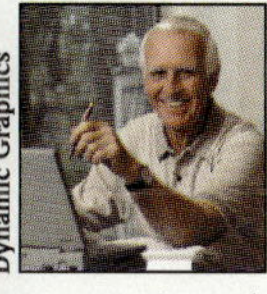

In childhood, the teacher decides what, when, and how the child will learn. But adults see themselves as self-directed and expect others to view them that way also. Adults want to decide for themselves what they will learn, when they will learn it, and how they will go about it. The teacher and adult student see each other as equals in a mutually helpful relationship.

■ *Adult learning goals are specific and more immediate.*

Dynamic Graphics

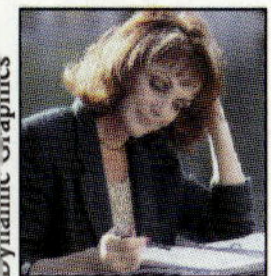

Children go to school to gain a broad understanding of subjects that will help them later in life. Their studies are one of postponed application. They are told, "Someday you'll need to know that."

Adults have a much different perspective. They read a book or enroll in a course looking for answers to specific problems, and they want to make immediate applications. We could say the child's learning is subject-centered, while the adult's learning is problem-centered.

An adult's greater life-experience is an important aid in learning.

DigitalVision

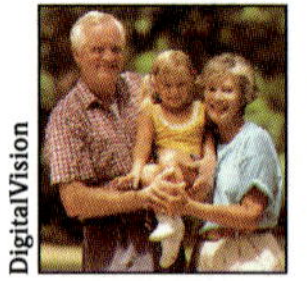

In childhood, the teacher's experience is the primary resource for learning. A child has limited experience. This makes the child more dependent on the teacher, and the learning situation is characterized more by one-way communication.

But for adults, everyone's experience and knowledge is valued as a resource. Adult students share their knowledge, and as a result everyone's learning is enriched; the teacher is not the sole contributor. Adults are more interdependent in their learning with multidirectional communication.

Adults group themselves for learning more on the basis of interest than on the basis of age-level.

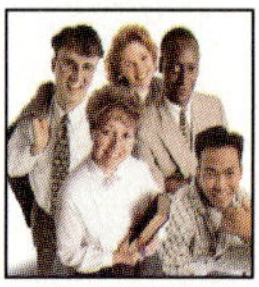
RubberBall

For children, decisions about grouping and curriculum are generally based on age. Certain subjects are deemed appropriate at a certain age. Adults are not as concerned about age; they gravitate toward other adults with similar concerns and interests. For example, a community education course on household maintenance and a church class on enriching your marriage are likely to have adults of a wide age-span. It is not the age but the subject that is important.

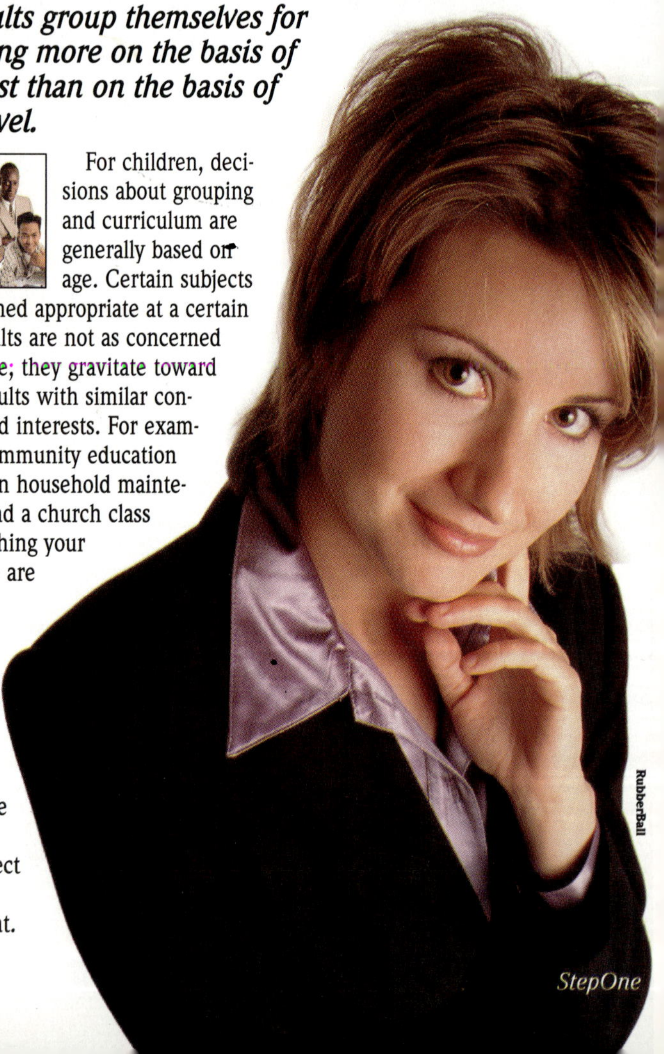
RubberBall

■ *Adults learn best when they are treated like adults.*

As James DeBoy observes, "If adults perceive that they are being treated as children or without respect (being talked down to or given simplistic explanations, with their questions ridiculed or ignored), they will not participate in such programs."

■ *Adults learn best when physically comfortable.*

Children can tolerate uncomfortable situations better than adults. Of course, children deserve the best conditions possible. But adults have little tolerance for discomfort.

The physical effects of aging inflict adults with a greater sensitivity. Muscles cramp and joints stiffen more easily. They get chilled or overheated. Extraneous noises can distract them. They need conditions consistent with their hearing and vision needs. Poor ventilation can cause drowsiness.

Adults are accustomed to quality treatment in the secular community, and expect the same in the church. Uncomfortable surroundings will hinder adult learning.

■ *Adults learn best when they feel accepted.*

The more the teacher does to build relationships with students and between students the more relaxed adults will be, and the more they will learn. Just as being a pastor has an element of teaching in it, so teaching a Sunday School class has an element of pastoral ministry. Spending time with adults and carefully listening to them will help them feel accepted. The sharing of burdens in prayer will also help bond the class together. Give opportunity for adults to react, question, and comment. If necessary, use small group techniques to do this. Adults also respond well to talking informally over light refreshments.

Comfortable settings and fellowship are not just "nice things to do"; they are essential in adult Christian education.

■ *All adults share some learning preferences.*

What do adults want? Studies and surveys of adults reveal the following expectations.
- They want a teacher who is a witness.
- They want the Bible lesson applied to everyday living.
- They want to attend a class that is nonthreatening.
- They want to talk. *Some do.*

Our adult classes can touch lives in powerful ways if we take the time to understand the uniqueness of adult education and shape our lessons and classrooms accordingly.

—*William P. Campbell*

Want to know more? Further information on this subject, can be found in *Focus on Adults* by William Campbell · ISBN 0-88243-407-1.

PREPARE YOURSELF

It is vital that teachers conduct a spiritual self-evaluation each week. Examine your life and attitude. If known sin exists in your life, repent and reestablish your commitment to be obedient to God's Word.

Next ask the Holy Spirit to guide your thoughts as you prepare. Remember, the Holy Spirit is the true teacher.

Finally, pray for the students you are going to teach. Ask God to prepare their hearts to be receptive to His truth.

MAKE THE LESSON YOURS

Before you read the prepared curriculum, read through the biblical text a few times.

On the first trip through the text, determine the main point of the biblical author. You must determine what the author was trying to say in order to communicate the principle to your class.

A primary objective of any teacher is to see his or her students excited about learning. One way a teacher can facilitate this is through effective lesson preparation.

You must know your audience if you wish to be an effective communicator.

On the next read through, determine how the main point impacted the original reader and his situation. To do that, look for situation clues. What appears to be going on in the society that caused the writer to make this point?

Finally, determine how the main point impacts you and your world. Ask yourself how the world situation has changed or stayed the same. What principles are transcultural? What demands will this principle place on the students in your classroom?

Now you should read through the commentary in the prepared curriculum for additional insights and methodologies that will help you communicate the truths of the passage.

KNOW THEIR WORLD

You must know your audience if you wish to be an effective communicator.

Be aware of your students' life situations. This information will help you tailor your lesson to meet their needs. Never manipulate the text to meet your goals, but use it to address relevant issues that are currently confronting your students.

BUILD A BRIDGE

Prepare an opening question related to the main point that will build a bridge between the world of the text and the world of the student. This question should identify a real-life problem that the text will answer.

Lead the group to the unknown (or the principles of the biblical text) through much the same process you used earlier to make the text your own.

Lead students back to their world by helping them make application of the biblical text to the problem identified earlier.

WALK IN OBEDIENCE

Help the group or individuals devise a plan to implement their application of the biblical lesson. And pray for the Holy Spirit to help in the process.

Develop accountability partners who will assist students to live out what they have learned. Each week, build in class time to allow students to share their spiritual successes.

Adults come to class because they want to learn. Take the time to properly prepare, then enjoy the fruit of your labor.

g Effective Lessons

TEACHING WITH *Style*

Effective teachers identify and understand various learning styles.

Many Sunday School teachers present Bible lessons using methods that appeal to their own learning style. Without giving the methods much thought, teachers make the unconscious assumption that their way of learning is the "right" way.

No matter the format or the class size, learning is an individual experience. Each student has a particular learning style, which may or may not be the same as the teacher's. Being able to identify and understand various learning styles and their importance will make a teacher more effective.

WHAT ARE LEARNING STYLES?

A learning style is the way a person sees or perceives things best, and how he or she processes or uses what has been seen. David Kolb and Bernice McCarthy have identified four basic types of learners.

■ IMAGINATIVE LEARNERS

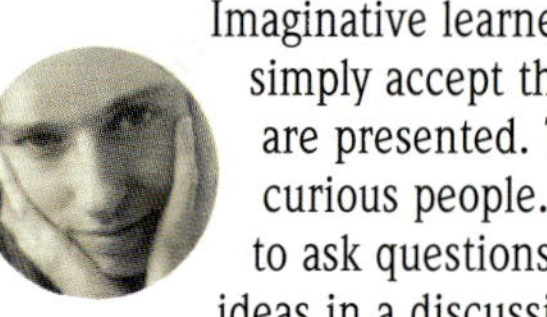

Imaginative learners do not simply accept things as they are presented. They are curious people. They want to ask questions and explore ideas in a discussion format. Most adults who learn this way are "big picture" people. They want to see how things work together to produce an overall result. They understand that there are many facets of any concept and are not satisfied until they have examined them all.

In addition to discussions, an effective way to teach an imaginative learner is through the use of role play and case study. These learners do not respond well to long lectures, memorizing, or working alone.

 ANALYTIC LEARNERS

Analytic learners are quite the opposite of imaginative learners. They like the lecture format, viewing the teacher as the primary information provider. The student's job is to analyze the information and pass judgment on it.

These learners value facts, figures, and the way it "should be." In addition to lectures, they enjoy debates, information sheets, and guest experts. They don't enjoy group activities.

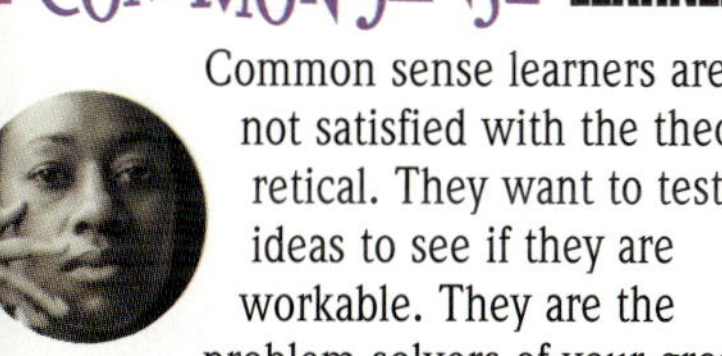 COMMON SENSE LEARNERS

Common sense learners are not satisfied with the theoretical. They want to test ideas to see if they are workable. They are the problem solvers of your group. They like to move while they learn, being hands-on learners who want to see results. The best way to teach these individuals is through practical demonstrations, testimonies, and projects.

DYNAMIC LEARNERS

Dynamic learners look at things with an eye to the future. They are creative and have a "what if?" mentality. They are risk-takers. The past is only important in as far as it leads to the future. They tend to be leaders. They also see the humor in situations. Flexibility is an important aspect of their learning style. They are typified by having many projects started but few finished.

These learners want a teacher who will facilitate rather than dictate. They enjoy drama, creative writing, or art projects that allow them to express themselves.

CREATING A BALANCED APPROACH

The wise teacher uses various methods so every student has an equal opportunity to learn God's Word. Using a creative mixture of methods allows the instructor to appeal to a variety of learning styles reaching the widest possible spectrum of students in relevant ways.

CREATING A *Growth* ENVIRONMENT

Many teachers wonder why more people don't come to their Sunday School classes. Others wonder why those who do come don't seem to respond in a positive manner. An answer to both of these questions is tied to the atmosphere or environment present in the classroom. Here are a few things that will help set the tone you need for a successful class.

TEACHER'S ATTITUDE

The most important factor in a successful Sunday School class is the teacher. If the teacher is not excited about being in the class, it is unlikely that the students will be excited.

There are a number of ways a teacher can communicate excitement. Being the first person in the classroom prepared to greet students says that you are glad that they came to share this experience.

Being prepared to teach each Sunday communicates the importance of learning and the learning process.

Presenting material in an enthusiastic manner, sharing how the biblical principles have impacted your life, and encouraging students to apply the principles in their own lives says that Bible study is more than the accumulation of historical facts.

SOCIAL CLIMATE

For a Sunday School class to be successful, the students must like each other and want to be together.

One of the best ways to foster a "family" feeling in the class is through outside social activities.

Potlucks are always good social events. So are trips to sporting events, going to concerts together, or getting together to play volleyball. Try to plan at least one outside class activity each month or at the very least once per quarter.

Always designate time during the class session for informal social interaction. This can include a prayer and praise time, but should also include informal interaction around coffee and donuts (or a more healthy alternative).

SAFE HAVEN

Adults want to share with one another during the

Sunday School hour. This is important, but it also presents a danger. Some class members may intentionally or unintentionally damage others with their comments or their reaction to someone else's comments.

It is the teacher's responsibility to make sure that

Being prepared each Sunday communicates the importance of learning.

Confidential information should be safeguarded.

everyone in the class is treated with respect and that each one's contribution is valued.

There will be times when a student's comments make little sense or do not contribute to the discussion. At those times, the teacher must take the initiative of acknowledging the response and turning the discussion back to the intended target.

Confidential information must also be safeguarded. Prayer requests and revelation of personal issues made in class should never be used against the person or as fodder for gossip. It is the teacher's responsibility to remind the class of this and to confront those who are in violation of group trust.

These are just a few ways you can create a growth environment. If you will do these things, you will have taken great strides in your journey toward developing a Sunday School class that will attract people and transform lives.

The teacher's attitude is a critical factor in the success of the class.

Foster a "family" feeling in the class through outside social activities.

Planning For Long-Term Results

Have you ever gotten lost because you thought you knew where you were going and failed to make proper preparation for the trip? This type of frustration is not limited to automobile drivers who don't plan. It is also typical of adult Sunday School teachers who try to arrive at the destination of good Christian education without mapping out a route to get there.

The Educational Map

Educational mapmaking is called "scope and sequencing." A scope and sequence is an educational device which allows the teacher to see the overall scope of his or her educational plan and the sequence (or steps to follow) to arrive successfully at his or her destination.

Without a scope and sequence, many adult Christian education classes seem aimless. A group finishes one course of study and then the teacher frantically looks around the local Bible bookstore for a topic that will captivate the group's attention for the next few weeks.

One of the advantages of an adult study group using dated curriculum such as *Radiant Life's Adult* or *Pathways For Young Adults* curriculum is that the editors of the curriculum have carefully developed the scope and sequence for them. Over a period of time, the dated curriculum covers a wide variety of topics presenting Scripture in a systematic fashion.

If the class has chosen to follow an elective-based Christian education program, it is vital for the teacher to develop his or her own scope and sequence. The advantage of this approach is that the teacher can tailor his or her educational map to reflect the specific needs of class members.

HOW DO YOU GO ABOUT CONSTRUCTING A SCOPE AND SEQUENCE?

1 **Develop a purpose statement** for your class based on the needs of your students and church and on the leading of the Holy Spirit.

2 **List various topics** that would meet the purpose statement that you have developed. Your list of topics should contain at least 10 to 15 offerings from the general areas of Bible book studies, practical Christian living, and Bible doctrine.

3 **Decide when each topic will be offered.** It is wise to think in 3-year blocks. This will provide you the opportunity to include 12 topics to accomplish your objective if you decide to offer one topic per quarter.

It is wise to stagger the type of courses you offer to insure variety and maintain the interest of the class. One way to do this is to offer an Old Testament book study followed by a topical study followed by a New Testament book study followed by a doctrinal study. Be creative as you develop a balanced sequence of studies to be offered.

4 **Examine various curriculum products.** Look for materials that are written from a Pentecostal perspective where possible. The titles found in Radiant Life's *Spiritual Discovery Series* and *Biblical Living Series* are excellent choices to meet this criterion. Preselecting your curriculum will save you from a last-minute scramble.

Following these four steps will help you advance toward your chosen destination with confidence. You will also be able to measure the distance you have progressed toward your objective.

Curriculum is a valuable teaching resource. Here are a few principles that will help you maximize its usefulness.

A Proper Perspective

Curriculum is a tool for the teacher; it is not the teacher. Some teachers simply read the curriculum commentary to the class each week. Although this may be a better option than going into a class and speaking in an uninformed fashion, it is not the preferred method of teaching.

Teachers should use curriculum as a base of operation. They must allow the Holy Spirit to direct them in tailoring the material found in the curriculum to the specific needs of their students.

Teachers should never think that they must use all of the activities included in the lesson.

A Flexible Resource

New teachers often become overwhelmed by the amount of material provided in curriculum. They feel there is no way they can use all the material in the typical 45 minutes of class time. They are right.

It is important for teachers to realize that an abundance of material is given in the curriculum intentionally to give the teacher a choice of teaching methods. Teachers should never think that they must use all of

Getting The Most Out Of

Throne Judgment (after the Millennium), the final resurrection of the wicked will take place. They will be thrown into the lake of [fire], and Christ's victory will be complete (see Revelation 21,22).

It will be a wonderful day when our bodies are transformed into immortal bodies. No longer will we be plagued with illnesses and normal aches and pains of life. We will become feeble or grow tired. Instead we live eternally with the Lord.

Our Victory

1 Corinthians 15:54-58

(Ask a student to read 1 Corinthians 15:54-58.) The transformation of our bodies will mark the victory of Christ over death once for all. Paul expressed the wonder of this event by quoting Isaiah 25:8 and Hosea 13:14. God will give complete victory (verses 56,57).

After this teaching of our future victory, Paul encouraged his readers to stand firm in their faith and to let nothing move them from their hope in Christ (verse 58). Because our work will be effective, we can work without reservation.

Notes

Easter is a time of celebration. Through His victory over death, Jesus paved the way for our salvation and resurrection. Because Jesus rose from the dead, we have the hopeful assurance that we will enjoy eternal life.

While Jesus is still at work conquering every enemy, we live in a tension between the partial victory He has given us and the complete victory that will soon be ours. This tension is often referred to as living in the now and the not yet. We have received salvation, but we still live in a fallen world. One day, however, our salvation will be complete, we will be transformed, and we will live eternally with Christ in His kingdom.

Since we have such a great hope, we can work for God without reservation. We know our future is in God's hands, a future that is wonderful beyond description. Therefore, we have nothing to fear, knowing our labor will not be in vain.

Through His sacrifice, Jesus paved the way for us to be reconciled to God. But we must confess our sins to Him and ask for His forgiveness. Encourage unsaved students to accept Christ today.

☐ Read study 9 in the Spring 2000 issue of the *Pathways Study Guide.* Note any information or questions you would like to use in class.

☐ Fill out a copy of the Planning The Session form (page 10) to ensure adequate time for the completion of each activity.

☐ Prepare copies of the work sheets "The God Of Miracles" and "Expect A Miracle" (*Pathways Resource Packet*, pages 32,33). Familiarize yourself with the content of these items prior to class.

☐ Make sure your classroom is equipped with an overhead projector, blank transparency, and transparency marker, or a chalkboard and chalk.

☐ Study 9 focuses on the ability and willingness of God to do miracles for His people today. Pray that the Lord will use this study to strengthen the faith of students who need a miracle.

14

Pathways Teac...

Focus:

God continues [to perform mira]cles today.

Objective

To recognize the [demon]strations of God's [love] and faithfulness i[n all situa]tions of life and [our need] for miraculous inte[rvention.]

Bible Text:

2 Kings 2:19-25; 4[:1-7,] 38-44; 6:1-7

Key Verse:

Jeremiah 32:20

NIV [You] perform miracul[ous s]igns and w[on]ders i[n E]gypt and ha[ve] continued them to t[his] day, both in Israel and among all mankind, and have gained the renow[n] that is still yours.

KJV Which hast set signs and wonders in the land of Egypt, even unto this day, and in Israel, and among other men; and hast made thee a name, as at this day.

D[istribute the] work sheet "The God Of Miracles." Instruct students to fill out the work sheet as you go through the study.)

? Ask: "How would you define or describe a miracle?" A miracle might be defined as supernatural, divine intervention into a situation that is otherwise impossible. God frequently performs a miracle when the situation seems most hopeless.

One factor common to miracles is the need for the exercise of faith in God. Jesus frequently commented on people's faith in connection with the miraculous. Also, miracles will bring glory to the Lord. Signs and wonders in the Bible were often granted as a means of causing people to glorify God. In today's study, we will examine six miracles [performed by ...]